westermann

W0399674

Level 7
Englisch

Übungsheft

INHALT

		SEITE
Kapitel 1:	**Food**	
	Listening	4
	Reading	6
	Writing	8
	Grammar – relative clauses	10
	Check	12
Kapitel 2:	**Health**	
	Listening	14
	Reading	16
	Writing	18
	Grammar – If-clauses	20
	Check	22
Kapitel 3:	**Activities**	
	Listening	24
	Reading	26
	Writing	28
	Grammar – quantities	30
	Check	32
Kapitel 4:	**Problems**	
	Listening	34
	Reading	36
	Writing	38
	Grammar – past progressive	40
	Check	42

Food

LISTENING (Seite 4–5)

1 What do you have for breakfast?

a) Richtig: 1.
b) Richtig: 1. + 3.

2 What is it?

1. C 2. G 3. A 4. F 5. B 6. D 7. E

3 Answer the questions.

1. tea 2. ham and cheese 3. bacon and eggs 4. curry/dinner from day before 5. the most important meal of the day 6. she's a vegetarian 7. hamburger or chips 8. this morning/in the morning

4 Lisa's and Ben's food

1. Lisa's breakfast: cup of tea 2. Ben's breakfast: 1 or 2 sandwiches with ham and cheese or some toast with jam 3. Lisa's snack at break: an apple 4. Ben's snack at break: – 5. Lisa's lunch: Where? cafeteria; What? lots of vegetables 6. Ben's lunch: Where? cafeteria; What? fast food, hamburger or chips

5 Over to you!

Eigene Antworten

READING (Seite 6–7)

1 The restaurant review

Richtig: 2. + 3.

2 What happened?

1. B 2. J 3. D 4. F 5. H 6. E 7. A 8. C 9. I 10. G

3 Questions about the review

1. four 2. last week 3. 7 p.m. 4. in the window, had flowers on it 5. another waiter 6. the price 7. it was cold 8. coffees 9. the brownie and the apple pie 10. no (he isn't)

WRITING (Seite 8–9)

1 Your opinion

Positive comments: I liked the table.; The waiter was very helpful.; Everyone found something they liked.; It wasn't too expensive.; I would recommend it to my friends.

Negative comments: I think the restaurant was terrible.; The food was cold.; There wasn't any choice.; The other guests were loud.; We waited a long time for the bill.

2 Opposites

1. expensive 2. bad 3. late 4. nice 5. fast 6. sad/unhappy 7. cold 8. quiet 9. negative 10. love/like 11. clean 12. small

3 A restaurant review

a) 1. B 2. H 3. F 4. D 5. A 6. G 7. C 8. E 9. I

GRAMMAR (Seite 10–11)

1 Relative clauses

a)

Paul:	Hi, my dad just booked a table for four. He is the man <u>who</u> forgot to leave his name.
Waiter:	Ah, yes. No, problem. We have three empty tables <u>which</u> are for four people. Come with me, please.
Paul:	Thank you.
Waiter:	What about this table <u>which</u> is by the window. There is a great view of the river <u>which</u> is very busy today. There are lots of people <u>who</u> are in their boats.
Paul:	This is a great table. Thank you. My parents will be here soon. They are parking our car.
Waiter:	Here are some menus. I'll come back when they arrive. This is the page <u>that</u> has today's specials on it.
Paul:	Great! Look here comes my family. The woman <u>that</u> is wearing the red coat is mum.
Waiter:	I'll go and meet them and bring them to the table.
Paul:	Thanks. And I'll look at the menu <u>that</u> is full of amazing dishes.

b) 1. This is the page which has today's specials on it. 2. The woman who is wearing the red coat is my mum. 3. And I'll look at the menu which is full of amazing dishes.

2 Who or which?

1. who 2. which 3. which 4. which 5. who 6. who

ISBN 978-3-14-121583-9

3 Word order
1. That is the man who delivers our pizzas. 2. That is the chef who cooks the best pizzas. 3. These are the pizzas which are the best pizzas in town. 4. This is the cheese which we always have on our pizzas. 5. The restaurant which is on the corner has the best pizzas.

4 What is it?
Lösungsvorschlag: 2. A teacher is a person who works at a school. 3. A menu is a book which has lots of food in it. 4. A waiter is a person who works in a restaurant. 5. Soup is a dish which you eat at the start of a meal.

CHECK (Seite 12–13)

1 Ordering food
1. Brendon 2. Brendon 3. Mum 4. Mum 5. Brendon, Mum 6. Brendon 7. Mum 8. Mum

2 The Benson family restaurant review
1. At Maya's Pizza and Pasta. 2. It was Mother's Day. 3. It was perfect. 4. Yes, they did. 5. No, there wasn't. 6. The mums got a flower and the dads got the bill.

3 A restaurant review
1. loud 2. nice 3. dark 4. expensive 5. helpful 6. hot 7. cold 8. late

4 Relative pronouns
1. who 2. who 3. which 4. which 5. which 6. who 7. who 8. which

Health

LISTENING (Seite 14–15)

1 Adrian's favourite sport
Richtig: 1. 2. 4. 5. 6. 8.

2 What are the numbers?
1. E 2. D 3. A 4. B 5. F 6. C

3 Complete the sentences.
1. BBC2 2. running 3. Camden Town 4. runners 5. every day 6. youngest 7. plan 8. sometimes

4 The right order
1. C 2. E 3. G 4. A 5. D 6. F 7. B

5 Over to you!
Eigene Antworten

READING (Seite 16–17)

1 Mark's visit to the doctor
Richtig: 2. 3. 4. 5.

2 Mark or Dr Baker?
1. Dr Baker + Mark 2. Dr Baker 3. Mark 4. Mark 5. Dr Baker 6. Dr Baker 7. Mark 8. Dr Baker 9. Mark 10. Dr Baker

3 What happened?
1. B 2. I 3. D 4. G 5. A 6. F 7. C 8. E 9. H

WRITING (Seite 18–19)

1 What's the problem?
a) Lösungsvorschlag: 1. eat too much 2. ride a bike (too fast) 3. rain 4. cut a banana A cut hand B stomach ache C hurt arm D have a cold E take medicine F need a bandage G stay in bed H drink tea and water/lots
b) 1. B, E, G, H 2. C, E, F, G 3. D, E, G, H 4. A, E, F

2 At the doctor's
Dialogue 1: 1 food 2 stomach ache 3 stay in bed 4 water
Dialogue 2: 1 What's the problem 2 fell off my bike 3 leg/arm hurts 4 medicine 5 bandage
Dialogue 3: 1 bad 2 a cold 3 stay in bed 4 lots of hot tea
Dialogue 4: 1 What's the problem 2 was cooking 3 cut my finger 4 medicine 5 bandage

GRAMMAR (Seite 20–21)

1 If-clauses
a) Paul: Dad, you need to do some sport. <u>If you do some sport, you won't feel tired.</u>
Dad: You're right. <u>If I go jogging in the park, I will listen to music, too.</u>
Paul: That's a good idea. <u>If you listen to music, you will have to be careful near the roads.</u>
Dad: Very true, but I won't listen to loud music.
Paul: What about swimming, too? <u>If you go swimming, I will come with you.</u> I love swimming.
Dad: I don't know. I don't like swimming much. We could cook some healthy meals.

ISBN 978-3-14-121583-9

Paul: If I write a shopping list, will you buy the things after work?
Dad: Of course. What can we cook tomorrow?
Paul: If I have time after my homework, I'll look for a new recipe.
Dad: Great! Tomorrow after work, I can go shopping. If the weather is good, I will go jogging. Then we can cook together. That's a good plan.
Paul: OK, now I have to do my homework.

b) 2. I will listen to music too if I go jogging in the park. 3. You will have to be careful near the roads if you listen to music. 4. I will come with you if you go swimming. 5. Will you buy the things after work if I write a shopping list? 6. I'll look for a new recipe if I have time after my homework. 7. I will go jogging if the weather is good.

2 If …

1. play … will win 2. will ask … have 3. rains … won't run 4. will eat … have 5. will go … don't feel 6. get … will get

3 Sentence chain

2. you will get ill. 3. you will go to the doctor. 4. she will give you a prescription. 5. you will have to take some medicine. 6. you won't be able to go to work.

4 Say it in English.

1. If my leg still hurts, I will go to the doctor. 2. If the weather is nice, we will have a picnic. 3. If we go on holiday, I'll go jogging every day. 4. If the doctor gives me advice, I'll listen to it.

CHECK (Seite 22–23)

1 Anna, the football player

1. wrong 2. right 3. right 4. wrong 5. right 6. right 7. wrong 8. right 9. right 10. wrong

2 What's wrong with Sarah?

1. football practice 2. yesterday/the day before 3. stay in bed and not do any sport 4. toast and tea 5. a football match 6. a broken arm

3 A healthy life

1. jogging 2. music 3. salad 4. chocolate 4. basketball 6. watch

4 If …

Richtige Teile: 1. am … will go 2. will tell … asks 3. will take … get 4. have to … will take 5. can't do … will understand 6. will write … can't go 7. can't go … will mail 8. miss … won't write

Activities

LISTENING (Seite 24–25)

1 What people do …

Richtig: 1. 3. 4. 8.

2 Who are they?

1. B 2. E 3. D 4. A 5. F 6. C

3 Complete the sentences.

1. doctor 2. school 3. work 4. young 5. dog 6. university 7. hospital 8. way

4 Information about the speakers

Mögliche Antworten: 1. works in (St Katherine's) hospital, watches TV all day 2. goes to school, helps her parents do the shopping, does her homework, relaxes 3. does the same things every day, gets up at 8 o'clock, has breakfast, takes his dog for a walk, has lunch, does the shopping, cleans the house, watches TV, goes to bed at 10 o'clock 4. does different things, goes for a long walk with her dog/Buddy, watches TV, listens to music, bakes a cake, sleeps, cleans the house, plays football, helps her children with their homework 5. works in a pub, works late on Saturdays, sleeps late on Sundays, works from 3 o'clock until 11 6. works in the hospital, helps people find their way, wears a green coat

5 Over to you!

Eigene Antworten

READING (Seite 26–27)

1 Celebration in town

1. costume 2. hat 3. lorry 4. fish and chips 5. big wheel 6. tickets

2 About the celebration weekend

1. B 2. H 3. E 4. F 5. A 6. I 7. D 8. G 9. C

ISBN 978-3-14-121583-9

3 Questions about the blog post
1. It's 100 years old. 2. They were dressed as people from 100 years ago and fishermen. 3. Hats are made in the town. 4. You could eat sweets, fish and chips, burgers and ice creams. 5. The tickets were for the train museum. 6. Because there isn't any school. 7. Tell her about how they celebrate. 8. eigene Antwort

WRITING (Seite 28–29)

1 A newspaper report
a) 1. E 2. A 3. H 4. C 5. F 6. B 7. D 8. G

2 Your newspaper report
a) eigene Antworten
b) Lösungsvorschlag: Last July there was a big concert in my town. The band 'Happy Socks' came back to their hometown and played in the park. Their music is great. There were food trucks in the park. They sold hot dogs, ice cream, smoothies and lots of other things. There was a competition to meet the band. Sarah Smith won two tickets and she had a great afternoon with the band. She had a tour of the stage and went for a meal at Angelo's Pizza Restaurant. The weather was nice all day, but it rained in the evening when the band went on stage. The concert was still really good.

GRAMMAR (Seite 30–31)

1 Quantities
a) There are a lot of things you can do this summer in Watchet. Our small town on the southwest coast of England has lots of activities and many of them are free. There isn't much time to write your name on the lists and there are limited places for some of the activities. There are many boats at Watchet. You can go on fishing trips, birdwatching or seal watching trips or you can help repair the boats – many of the owners need help all year.
There is a train museum in Watchet with a lot of old trains, old tickets and many other train things. It doesn't cost much money and you can spend all day in the museum. There is a café, too. Or you can help on the old train that takes a lot of visitors from Minehead to Taunton. You can check tickets or help in the restaurant kitchen.
If you like sport, there are many different sports activities. You can play football, rugby, hockey, go on bike tours of the area or learn to surf or sail a boat.
There is so much to do in Watchet you won't be bored this summer. Tell your friends and have fun. How many activities can you do? How much time have you got?
b) 1. There are lots of things you can do. 2. It doesn't cost much money. 3. How many activities can you do? 4. How much time have you got?

2 Much or many?
much: water, money, time, sugar, bread, weight
many: bottles, eggs, people, activities, sheep, sports

3 Activities week
1. many 2. Many/A lot of 3. much 4. a lot of 5. many / a lot of 6. much

4 Say it in English.
1. We don't have much time today. 2. How much money do you need for the trip? 3. How many activities can you do? 4. There was a lot of sand in my shoes after the walk on the beach. 5. I didn't know many people on the bike ride.

CHECK (Seite 32–33)

1 Gillian's weekend
1. E 2. C 3. F 4. A 5. D 6. G 7. B

2 Sarah's blog post
1. at 7:30 a.m. 2. good 3. went to London, went on the London Eye and visited the Tower of London (had a special tour) 4. volunteers at the food bank and homeless people 5. Yes, she did. 6. went on a boat trip on the Thames

3 A report
1. school's birthday 2. great 3. steaks 4. salads 5. cakes 6. ice cream 7. food trucks 8. competitions 9. presentations 10. rain

4 Quantities
1. many/a lot of 2. much 3. many 4. a lot of/many 5. a lot of/much 6. many 7. much 8. a lot of

Problems

LISTENING (Seite 34–35)

1 Brendon and Chris
Richtig: 2. 3. 5. 6. 8.

ISBN 978-3-14-121583-9

2 What happened?
1. F 2. C 3. H 4. D 5. B 6. A 7. E 8. I 9. G

3 Answer the questions.
1. b) 2. b) 3. a) 4. c) 5. c) 6. a) + b)

4 All about Chris
Used to live in: Beonstoke, small village, in the north of England, twenty miles from Liverpool
Now lives in: London
Where he lives is: really busy and street is quite loud
How he got to his old school: on foot
How he now gets to school: by bus
Likes: shops (many special offers)

5 Over to you!
Eigene Antworten

READING (Seite 36–37)

1 What's the problem?
Richtig: 1. 4. 5.

2 Jo or Mark?
1. Jo 2. Mark 3. Jo + Mark 4. Jo + Mark 5. Jo 6. Mark 7. Jo 8. Jo 9. Mark 10. Mark

3 Questions about the emails
1. Jo wants a cat. 2. She lives in a flat (without a garden). 3. They go to work. 4. She writes about a cat, dog, mouse (mice) and a rabbit. 5. He talks about an animal home. 6. You can take them for a walk.

4 Correct the sentences.
1. Jo has a **big** problem. 2. Dogs **are a lot of** work. 3. Cats **need to go outside**./ Cats **can't** stay inside all day. 4. You can **take the dogs for a walk** in an animal home.

WRITING (Seite 38–39)

1 An email
a) 1. B 2. F 3. H 4. A 5. E 6. C 7. G 8. D

2 Your email (Lösungsvorschlag)
a) Information in email: horrible messages on mobile phone, help from friend
Karim's questions: Can you help me, please? Can I find out who sends the messages? Will I be in trouble? Will my parents take my phone off me? What can I do?
Your ideas: talk to tutor/teachers/parents, talk about it in class
b) Dear Karim, Remember: It's not your fault. Tell your tutor, teachers and your parents. Talk about it in class. Maybe others get similar messages. You won't be in trouble. You haven't done anything wrong. Your parents will look at your phone, but you will keep it. Together you will stop these messages.

GRAMMAR (Seite 40–41)

1 The past progressive
a) Dear Karen,
When I <u>was talking</u> to you last night there was a loud noise. Did you hear it? I thought it was the cat.
Me and Noah <u>were looking</u> for the cat and we found a mouse. It <u>was eating</u> some cheese under the table. The cat wasn't anywhere. Then we heard it. It wasn't happy.
We looked everywhere. Where <u>was it sitting</u>? Have a guess. It <u>wasn't eating</u> its food. It <u>was hiding</u> in the cupboard next to the table. It looked very scared.
"What <u>are you doing</u>?" Noah asked. The cat was happy to see us.
I think the cat <u>was waiting</u> to catch the mouse. The mouse saw the cat and closed the cupboard door.
What <u>was the mouse doing</u> after we found the cat?
It <u>was eating</u> cheese under the table. I'm sure it <u>was smiling</u>.
Bye!

b) 1. (Vorschlag) It was eating some cheese under the table. 2. (Vorschlag) It wasn't eating or looking for food. 3. (Vorschlag) Where was it sitting?

2 Was or were?
1. was 2. was 3. were 4. were 5. were 6. Was

3 Negative sentences
1. Sarah wasn't talking to Karen. 2. The mouse wasn't watching the cat. 3. Sarah and Noah weren't looking for the cat. 4. The cat and mouse weren't sitting in the kitchen.

4 What were they doing?
2. What was Anna doing in the park? 3. Were you watching TV this morning? 4. Were the friends eating crisps? 5. What was Anna doing last night? 6. What was Sam doing at 12 a.m?

ISBN 978-3-14-121583-9

CHECK (Seite 42–43)

1 Robinson Crusoe
1. F 2. A 3. E 4. G 5. B 6. C 7. D

2 Sam's problem
1. Sam's parents are **splitting up**. 2. Sam and his brother don't **know what to do**. 3. First they should write **a list of questions**. 4. Then they should **talk to their parents**. 5. They can also talk **to friends whose parents have split up**. 6. They should remember **their parents still love them and it isn't their fault.**

3 An email
1. best friend 2. brown hair 3. sport 4. films 5. girlfriend 6. my feelings 7. spend time 8. like her

4 Say it in English.
1. They were watching a good film on TV. 2. My friend was walking in the park when she saw me. 3. It wasn't raining when I left the house. 4. We weren't sitting in the bus when it started. 5. What were you doing last night?

Inventions

LISTENING (Seite 44–45)

1 Welcome to our village
Richtig: 2. 3. 5. 6. 8.

2 What is at the village?
1. G 2. A 3. E 4. F 5. B 6. D 7. C

3 About the village
1. right 2. right 3. wrong 4. right 5. wrong 6. wrong 7. right 8. right 9. wrong 10. right

4 Complete the sentences.
1. welcomes 2. villages 3. farmhouses 4. history 5. classes 6. fire 7. drink 8. birthday

5 Over to you!
Eigene Antworten

READING (Seite 46–47)

1 The Transport Museum
1. coach 2. boat/ship 3. wheel 4. plane 5. helicopter 6. motorbike

2 About the museum
1. A-E 2. E 3. A 4. E 5. D 6. C 7. B 8. B 9. C

3 Questions about the museum
1. everyone 2. on the top floor and the third floor 3. a paper plane/helicopter 4. the bikes and motorbikes 5 yes 6. on every floor 7. posters, postcards, pens, books and films about the museum 8. tour guides 9. five 10. nothing

WRITING (Seite 48–49)

1 Inventions
a) 1. B 2. E 3. D 4. A 5. F 6. C
b) 1. matches 2. car 3. chocolate chip cookies 4. light bulb 5. telephone 6. dishwasher

2 About the inventions
a) (Lösungsvorschlag) 1. Thomas Edison invented the light bulb in 1879. He came from the USA. The light bulb was used to light rooms and streets. 2. Cars were invented by Karl Benz. He lived in Germany. Cars are used to travel long distances. 3. Josephine Cochrane, from the USA, invented the dishwasher. It is used for washing plates, cups and glasses. It was invented in 1886. 4. John Walker invented matches in 1826. They are used to make fire. He came from England. 5. The telephone was invented by Alexander Graham Bell in Scotland in 1876. It is used to talk to people far away. I think it is a great invention. 6. Ruth Wakefield invented chocolate chip cookies in 1930. She came from the USA. They make your sweet tooth happy when you eat them.
b) eigene Antwort

GRAMMAR (Seite 50–51)

1 The passive
a) The first car <u>was invented</u> in 1672. Then different inventors tried different ideas and in 1887 Carl Benz developed a car and several of them <u>were made</u>. In 1908 the Ford Motor Company produced the Ford Model T which <u>was</u> the first car <u>made</u> in a big factory. Lots of people worked on assembly lines. Many of the same car <u>were made</u> every day.
People wanted to travel, and they all wanted a car. Cars <u>were bought</u> in their thousands and roads <u>were built</u> everywhere.
Nowadays electricity <u>is used</u> instead of petrol. This protects the environment. Cars <u>are used</u> a lot, maybe we should all walk more.

ISBN 978-3-14-121583-9

b) 1. The first car was invented in 1672. 2. Several of them were made. 3. Many of the same car were made every day. 4. Cars were bought in their thousands. 5. Roads were built everywhere. 6. Nowadays electricity is used. 7. Cars are used a lot.

2 Past participles

1. brought 2. drunk 3. eaten 4. got 5. given 6. gone 7. had 8. known 9. made 10. put 11. taken 12. written

3 What do you know?

1. Cakes **are made** with butter, sugar, flour and eggs. 2. Stamps **are used** on letters. 3. Food **is bought** in supermarkets. 4. Cars **are driven** by people over 18. 5. Roads **are built** to connect towns. 6. Fish **are caught** in rivers and the sea.

4 Famous inventions

1. The light bulb **was used** first to light rooms and streets. 2. People **were spoken** to on the telephone for the first time in 1876. 3. Matches **were invented** by John Walker. 4. Cars **were built** to travel long distances on roads. 5. Plates **were washed** by hand before dishwashers **were invented**. 6. Mobiles **were developed** so you can take them with you.

CHECK (Seite 52–53)

1 Important inventions

1. B + D 2. C + F 3. A + E

2 The best smartphone

1. It is about a smartphone. 2. The photos are amazing. 3. You don't lose your photos or films. 4. It is white. 5. You can save your own music. 6. You can make phone calls.

3 A great invention

1. watch 2. living room 3. small 4. change 5. behind 6. films 7. stream 8. television 9. black 10. colour

4 Inventions you know

1. Windows **are made** of glass. 2. Computers **are sold** everywhere. 3. Apps **are uploaded** onto mobile devices. 4. The telephone **was invented** in 1876. 5. Our television **was bought** last year. 6. Our house **was built** in 2000. 7. Microwaves **are used** to warm food. 8. My bike **was stolen** from the park.

Holidays

LISTENING (Seite 54–55)

1 Which summer camp is right for you?

Richtig: 1. 2. 4. 5.

2 Which summer camp is it?

1. C, F 2. D, E, G 3. A, E 4. B, H

3 Answer the questions.

1. Around the UK. 2. Sports clubs. 3. His football club. 4. Manchester. 5. Take them home./Show your friends and family. 6. Work on them on the computer. 7. Keep it clean and tidy. 8. Leave it alone.

4 Information about summer camps

1. Sports camp
Others there: other teams
Activities: train, practise your favourite sport, train together, play matches, swimming, sightseeing, cinema
2. Film making camp
Others there: –
Activities: learn how to make cool films, write a story, learn how to work with a camera, make film into real film on camera, learn how to cut and edit your film
3. Art camp
Others there: artisits, painters, photographers, sculptors
Activities: see new ways to draw, how to work with stone and other kinds of things, painting, taking nice photos, work on photos on computer

5 Over to you!

Eigene Antworten

READING (Seite 56–57)

1 Holidays

1. Cornwall 2. Loch Ness 3. London

2 Anna's holiday

Loch Ness

3 Which holiday place?

1. A, C, E, H 2. B, C, F, I 3. A, B, C, D, G

ISBN 978-3-14-121583-9

4 Questions about the holidays
1. You can see views of the city. 2. You know them from the TV. 3. No one has a problem with the food (in London). 4. Loch Ness is a lake and a monster. 5. In restaurants at Loch Ness. 6. You can take time out from city life or life itself. 7. In the southwest of England. 8. There are shops. 9. You can stay in hotels or holiday cottages. 10. eigene Antwort

WRITING (Seite 58–59)

1 A blog post
a) 1. A 2. G 3. D 4. B 5. H 6. F 7. C 8. E

2 A blog post comment
a) 1. Where are you going? What do you want to see? How did you plan everything? 2. No, they aren't. 3. You should be polite. 4. That the blogger walks the dogs at the animal home on Saturdays.
b) eigene Antwort

GRAMMAR (Seite 60–61)

1 Modal verbs
a) I'm really looking forward to our holiday. Scotland is a special place. We just have to remember there are rules there: in the museums and castles, in the hotels and also in restaurants. Of course, I know in restaurants you should be quiet and polite to everyone. In museums and castles, you shouldn't run or shout, you should only eat and drink in the special areas and you aren't allowed to take photos in some places. In the last hotel we stayed in I was allowed to look in the kitchen and I was able to watch the cook, that was fun. I wasn't allowed to cook any food for hotel guests. I'd like to be a cook when I leave school.
b) Things Samira can do: have to remember there are rules, be quiet and polite to everyone in restaurants, only eat and drink in special areas in museums and castles, look in the kitchen, watch the cook
Things Samira can't do: run and shout in museums and castles, take photos in some places, cook any food for hotel guests

2 The right word
1. couldn't 2. must 3. couldn't / wasn't able to 4. isn't allowed to / can't 5. has to 6. mustn't / aren't allowed to

3 What are the rules?
2. The kids aren't allowed to take chips in the shop. 3. You are allowed to go and look around the garden. 4. Sarah isn't allowed to play music after 10 o'clock. 5. You aren't allowed to use your mobile phones in the restaurant. 6. Mark is only allowed to have one piece of cake. / Mark is allowed a piece of cake, but only one.

CHECK (Seite 62–63)

1 Airport announcements
1. 10:15 2. Berlin 3. 4D 4. 12:30 5. 30 minutes 6. 10:30 7. 5 minutes 8. Berlin

2 Sarah's postcard
1. Sam 2. Wales 3. visited the castle and the stadium 4. went hiking 5. fishing in the sea 6. fish and chips

3 A blog post
1. weekend 2. swimming pool 3. too old 4. seat 5. wouldn't move 6. ice cream 7. weekend 8. problems

4 Say it in English.
1. You shouldn't take any photos. 2. We mustn't eat chips in the castle. 3. Are we allowed to/May we go fishing? 4. We must stay on the paths in the mountains. 5. I'm not allowed to take any sand home from the beach. 6. I am able to/can speak English and French.

ISBN 978-3-14-121583-9

		SEITE
Kapitel 5:	**Inventions**	
	Listening	44
	Reading	46
	Writing	48
	Grammar – passive	50
	Check	52
Kapitel 6:	**Holidays**	
	Listening	54
	Reading	56
	Writing	58
	Grammar – modal verbs	60
	Check	62
	Bildquellen	64
	Trackliste	64
	Lösungen	Einleger

Digital+

Digitale Ergänzungen zu deinem Arbeitsheft erkennst du an dem Digital+ Symbol. Dazu zählen Audios und Videos. Gehe auf ***www.westermann.de/webcode*** und gib den gewünschten Webcode ein (z. B. WES-121583-001). Du kannst auch den QR-Code scannen.

Food

Tipp

Nicht vergessen: Du darfst den Hörtext vor jeder Aufgabe nochmal hören und danach ein weiteres Mal, um deine Antworten zu prüfen.

Audio: WES-121583-001

1 What do you have for breakfast?

a) What does Lisa have for breakfast? Tick ☑ the right things.

1. ☐

2. ☐

3. ☐

b) What does Ben have for breakfast? Tick ☑ the right things.

1. ☐

2. ☐

3. ☐

2 What is it?

Match the food with the right description.

1. sandwich
2. toast
3. English breakfast
4. vegetarian food
5. curry
6. fast food
7. breakfast

A bacon and eggs
B Indian food
C ham and cheese
D hamburger or chips
E important meal
F lots of vegetables
G jam

1	2	3	4	5	6	7
C						

Tipp

Während du das Interview hörst, beantworte die Fragen in Übung 3 oder ergänze die Informationen in Übung 4 mit Notizen. Höre dir das Interview ein weiteres Mal an und prüfe deine Antworten. Korrigiere falsche Antworten in einer anderen Farbe.

3 Answer the questions.

Answer the questions with information from the interview.

1. What drink does Lisa have for breakfast? ______
2. What does Ben have in his sandwiches? ______
3. What does Ben say is in a cooked breakfast? ______
4. What does Ben sometimes eat for breakfast? ______
5. What does Ben's dad say about breakfast? ______
6. Why does Lisa eat lots of vegetables? ______
7. What does Ben say is fast food? ______
8. When was the interview? ______

4 Lisa's and Ben's food

Complete the information.

1. Lisa's breakfast: ______
2. Ben's breakfast: ______
3. Lisa's snack at break: ______
4. Ben's snack at break: ______
5. Lisa's lunch: Where? ______
   What? ______
6. Ben's lunch: Where? ______
   What? ______

5 Over to you!

Write what you eat.

Your breakfast: ______

Your snack at break: ______

Your lunch: ______

Your evening meal: ______

Your favourite food: ______

Tipp

Um den Text besser zu verstehen, kannst du wichtige Textstellen unterstreichen.

Joe's Vegetarian Diner ★★★★☆

It was my birthday yesterday and we decided to go to the new vegetarian restaurant in town – Joe's Vegetarian Diner. There was a report about it last week in the newspaper. We aren't vegetarians, but we thought we'd try it. I booked a table online for four people for 7 p.m. We were a bit early, but our table was ready. It was in the window so we could watch the world outside and enjoy our meal. There were real flowers on the table, and it looked very nice.

We ordered some drinks which the waiter brought very quickly. We had some questions about some of the meals on the menu. There was only one question that the waiter couldn't answer, after asking another waiter he could tell us what we wanted to know. He recommended a dish that wasn't on the menu but was a special yesterday. He even told us the price of the dish – that doesn't always happen. I ordered the special.

Everybody's food arrived at the same time. Nothing was missing and there was lots to eat. After about five minutes our waiter returned to check everything was OK. We needed some more drinks which he brought very quickly.

We really enjoyed our main courses and we thought a dessert was a good idea. There wasn't a big choice, but we all found something we liked. Unfortunately, they forgot the cream on my brownie and the apple pie was cold. We told the waiter, and he brought a dish of cream and some warm apple pie with ice cream.

After coffees we asked for the bill which was also a nice surprise. The brownie and the apple pie weren't on the bill. We asked the waiter, and he said, "You weren't happy, so you don't have to pay."

I recommend this restaurant to everyone – vegetarian or not – and I might even give it five stars instead of four next time.

Dave, the non-vegetarian who loved a vegetarian restaurant ☺

1 The restaurant review

Read the review. Which pictures match the review?

1. ☐

2. ☐

3. ☐

Tipp

Jetzt bearbeite diese Aufgaben. Du kannst den Text immer wieder durchlesen, um deine Antworten zu prüfen.

2 What happened?

Put the things in the right order.

A They ordered their meals.

B Joe's Vegetarian Diner opened.

C They told the waiter about the problems with their desserts.

D Dave booked a table online.

E They asked some questions about things on the menu.

F Dave and his guests arrived at the restaurant.

G Dave wrote the review.

H They ordered their drinks.

I They paid the bill.

J There was a report about the restaurant in the newspaper.

1	2	3	4	5	6	7	8	9	10
B									

3 Questions about the review

Answer the questions with information from the review.

1. How many stars did Dave give the restaurant? ____________________
2. When was the report in the newspaper? ____________________
3. What time did Dave book the table for? ____________________
4. Describe the table. (Two things) ____________________
5. Who did the waiter ask for help? ____________________
6. What information did the waiter give about the special? ____________________
7. What was wrong with the apple pie? ____________________
8. What did they have after dessert? ____________________
9. What wasn't on the bill? ____________________
10. Is Dave a vegetarian? ____________________

Tipp

Für manche Textformen gibt es einen besonderen Wortschatz. Du lernst am besten die Ausdrücke auswendig.

1 Your opinion

Write the sentences in the right group.

I liked the table. | I think the restaurant was terrible. | The food was cold. | There wasn't any choice. | The waiter was very helpful. | The other guests were loud. | Everyone found something they liked. | It wasn't too expensive. | I would recommend it to my friends. | We waited a long time for the bill.

Positive comments ☺	Negative comments ☹

2 Opposites

Write the opposites of these words. They might be useful when you write a restaurant review.

1. cheap ↔ ______
2. good ↔ ______
3. early ↔ ______
4. terrible ↔ ______
5. slow ↔ ______
6. happy ↔ ______
7. hot ↔ ______
8. loud ↔ ______
9. positive ↔ ______
10. hate ↔ ______
11. dirty ↔ ______
12. big ↔ ______

Tipp

1. Bevor du anfängst solltet du dir überlegen, was du schreiben möchtest.
2. Mache einen Entwurf.
3. Schreibe dein Text.
4. Lasse jemand anderes deinen Text kontrollieren.
5. Schreibe deinen Text fehlerfrei ab.

3 A restaurant review

a) Put the parts of the restaurant review in the right order.

A	The restaurant was very loud, and the waiter wasn't very helpful. He didn't listen to my order and brought me the wrong drink.	
B	Fiona's Diner ★★☆☆☆	
C	I didn't order a dessert. When the bill came there was a starter on it that I didn't order or eat.	
D	My table was in a dark corner at the back of the restaurant.	
E	The waiter didn't believe me, and I spoke to the manager. He said, "Sorry!" and I didn't pay for my meal.	
F	I have been there before, and it was always very good.	
G	My steak wasn't cooked, there was a hair in my salad and my chips were cold.	
H	I had a horrible meal at Fiona's Diner last night.	
I	I can't recommend Fiona's Diner and I won't go there again. Claire, not happy and hungry	

1	2	3	4	5	6	7	8	9
B								

b) Write the restaurant review in the correct order.

Language Tip

Mit **Relativsätzen** kannst du eine Person oder eine Sache näher beschreiben. Ein **Relativsatz** beginnt meist mit einem Relativpronomen: **who**, **which** oder **that**.

Someone who plays football must be fit.	Jemand, der Fußball spielt, muss fit sein.
There are many **tourists who** take photos.	Es gibt viele Touristen, die Fotos machen.
They are listening to a **band which** is playing good music.	Sie hören ein Band, die tolle Musik spielt.
I've got a **computer game which** is really good.	Ich habe ein Computerspiel, das richtig gut ist.

Das **Relativpronomen that** kannst du sowohl für **Personen** als auch für **Dinge** benutzen.

There are lots of **people that** dance to our music.	Es gibt viele Menschen, die zu unserer Musik tanzen.
Ice hockey is a **sport that** can be dangerous.	Eishockey ist ein Sport, der gefährlich sein kann.

Video: WES-121583-002

1 Relative pronouns

a) Read the text and underline all the *relative pronouns*.

Paul:	Hi, my dad just booked a table for four. He is the man <u>who</u> forgot to leave his name.
Waiter:	Ah, yes. No, problem. We have three empty tables which are for four people. Come with me, please.
Paul:	Thank you.
Waiter:	What about this table which is by the window. There is a great view of the river which is very busy today. There are lots of people who are in their boats.
Paul:	This is a great table. Thank you. My parents will be here soon. They are parking our car.
Waiter:	Here are some menus. I'll come back when they arrive. This is the page that has today's specials on it.
Paul:	Great! Look here comes my family. The woman that is wearing the red coat is my mum.
Waiter:	I'll go and meet them and bring them to the table.
Paul:	Thanks. And I'll look at the menu that is full of amazing dishes.

b) Rewrite these sentences from the text. Replace *that* with *who* or *which*.

1. This is the page that has today's specials on it.

____

2. The woman that is wearing the red coat is my mum.

____

3. And I'll look at the menu that is full of amazing dishes.

____

2 Who or which?

Complete the sentences. Do you need *who* or *which*?

1. Sarah? She's the girl ______________________________ doesn't eat meat.
2. The vegetables ______________________________ I really like, are carrots and mushrooms.
3. Apples are the fruit ______________________________ are green, red, yellow or all three colours.
4. We buy our food from the market ______________________________ is in the middle of town.
5. The man ______________________________ has the cheese stand always sells us great cheese.
6. The butcher ______________________________ sells meat and eggs is my uncle.

3 Word order

Put the sentences in the correct order.

1. our pizzas / who delivers / that is the man

____

2. who cooks / that is the chef / the best pizzas

____

3. which are / the best pizzas in town / these are the pizzas

____

4. which we always / this is the cheese / have on our pizzas

____

5. has the best pizzas / which is on the corner / the restaurant

____

4 What is it?

Explain these things. Use *who* or *which*?

1. carrots: Carrots are a vegetable which are orange.
2. teacher: ____
3. menu: ____
4. waiter: ____
5. soup: ____

Audio: WES-121583-003

1 Ordering food

Listen to the dialogue. Who eats which food? Tick ✓.

	Brendon	Mum
1. a hot curry	☐	☐
2. chicken and rice	☐	☐
3. a vegetarian dish	☐	☐
4. potato curry	☐	☐
5. cheese balls	☐	☐
6. chilli chicken	☐	☐
7. Indian milk balls	☐	☐
8. vanilla ice cream	☐	☐

2 The Benson family restaurant review

Maya's Pizza and Pasta ★★★★★
What can I say? This place is amazing. We went for Mother's Day.
We had soup, pizza, pasta, salad and ice cream and everything was perfect.
The kids had pictures and puzzles and were very happy. The food came quickly. It was hot ... well the salad and ice cream was cold. ☺ The prices are very family friendly. The waiters are Italian, helpful and loved the kids. We were two families which was no problem for the bill – each family got a bill. All the mums got a flower, and the dads got the bill.
The Benson family, very happy customers

Read the restaurant review and answer the questions. Write complete sentences.

1. Where did the Benson family eat? __________
2. What was the special day? __________
3. What was the food like? __________
4. Did the kids like the restaurant? __________
5. Was there a problem with the bill? __________
6. What did the mums and dads get? __________

3 A restaurant review

Complete the restaurant review. Use the information in the box.

food:	cold, late, expensive
restaurant:	dark, loud, hot
waiter:	helpful, nice

The best place in town ★☆☆☆☆

I don't understand how this place got its name. We didn't like it. It was very (1) ________________ and the (2) ________________ waiter couldn't hear our order. We couldn't read the menus because it was very (3) ________________ and we couldn't see the (4) ________________ prices – that was good. We had some questions, and the waiter was very (5) ________________ . He asked the chef when he didn't know the answers. We waited 30 minutes for our food in a very (6) ________________ restaurant, and it was (7) ________________ when it came. We told the waiter, and it was very (8) ________________ when our hot food came.

We won't go again, and I won't recommend it to my friends.

Sam

4 Relative pronouns

Complete the sentences. Do you need *who* or *which*?

1. My English teacher, ________________ is American, has a funny accent.
2. That's the shop assistant ________________ is always helpful.
3. That's the restaurant ________________ we went to on my birthday.
4. That chocolate, ________________ you bought me, is great.
5. The dog, ________________ lives down the road, is old.
6. She's the police officer ________________ came to school about the accident.
7. My mum's sister, ________________ is my aunt, has opened a restaurant.
8. This vegetarian food, ________________ is not meat, tastes really good.

Health

Tipp

Die Informationen, die du für die Aufgaben brauchst, sind immer in der gleichen Reihenfolge wie es in dem Hörtext vorkommt.

Audio: WES-121583-004

1 Adrian's favourite sport

What does Adrian talk about? Tick ✓ the right things.

1. ☐

2. ☐

3. ☐

4. ☐

5. ☐

6. ☐

7. ☐

8. ☐

2 What are the numbers?

Match the numbers with the information.

1. 14
2. 11
3. 3 or 4
4. 26
5. 13
6. 5

A how often a week the group trains
B a marathon
C miles in race Adrian ran in
D Adrian's age when he started running
E Adrian's age now
F a half marathon

1	2	3	4	5	6
E					

Tipp

Die Hörtexte sind jetzt etwas länger. Keine Panik! Du kannst auf Pause gehen, einen Teil der Aufgabe machen und dann weiterhören. Höre dir den Text dann noch einmal komplett an.

3 Complete the sentences.

Complete the sentences. Underline the right words.

1. *My Sports* is a radio programme on BBC1 / BBC2 .
2. Adrian really likes runner / running .
3. Adrian lives in Camden Town / Regent's Park .
4. He runs in Regent's Park with a group of runners / friends .
5. Adrian trains every Monday / every day .
6. Adrian is the youngest / oldest in his running group.
7. Adrian has his own training plan / planner .
8. After school Adrian is sometimes / often tired.

4 The right order

Put the information in the right order.

A best runner in group

B London Marathon

C started running and never stopped

D Adrian in interview on BBC2

E 5-mile race

F Half marathon

G people cheered and gave him energy

1	2	3	4	5	6	7
C						

5 Over to you!

Write about your favourite sport.

What? ______________________________

Where? ______________________________

Who with? ______________________________

How often? ______________________________

Why? ______________________________

Tipp

Einen Dialog musst du aufmerksam lesen. Du kannst ihn mehrmals lesen, um zu unterscheiden, wer was sagt.

Mark: Good morning, Dr Baker.

Dr Baker: Good morning, Mark. What's the problem?

Mark: My arm is swollen, and it really hurts.

Dr Baker: What happened?

Mark: I was playing football in the park yesterday and I fell. I landed on my arm, and it really hurt.

Dr Baker: It looks broken. Let's take an X-ray and find out. Go with the nurse and I'll see you again when we have some pictures of your arm.

Mark: OK, thank you.

Dr Baker: So, Mark your elbow is broken but the bones haven't moved. Look at the X-ray picture. You need a bandage from your hand to your shoulder. It will take six weeks to get better.

Mark: Six weeks? What about sport?

Dr Baker: You can't play football for six weeks and after that you have to be very careful. Your muscles won't be very strong.

Mark: OK. Thank you, Dr Baker.

Dr Baker: Here is a prescription for some medicine. Take the medicine and your arm won't hurt anymore. Come again next week and we can take another X-ray to check your arm.

Mark: It's my left arm and I write with my right hand so I can still go to school.

Dr Baker: That's good, Mark. Get well soon! See you next week.

1 Mark's visit to the doctor

Read the dialogue. Which pictures match the dialogue?

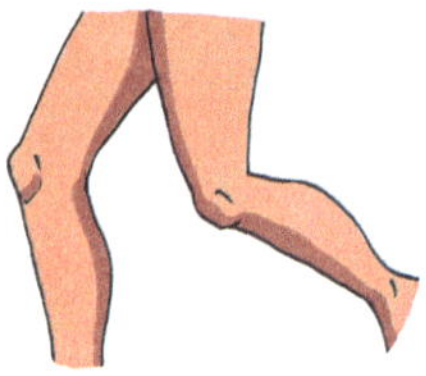

1. ☐

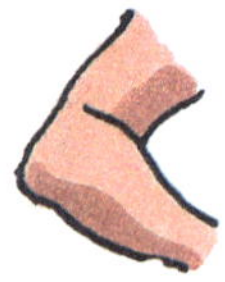

2. ☐

3. ☐

4. ☐

5. ☐

6. ☐

Tipp

Probiere mal die Aufgaben zu lösen und kontrolliere danach deine Antworten mit dem Dialog auf Seite 16. Konntest du dich an alles erinnern?

2 Mark or Dr Baker?

Who said what? Match the things with the right person.

	Mark	Dr Baker
1. Good morning.	☐	☐
2. What happened?	☐	☐
3. I was playing football in the park.	☐	☐
4. I landed on my arm.	☐	☐
5. Let's take an X-ray.	☐	☐
6. Your elbow is broken.	☐	☐
7. Six weeks?	☐	☐
8. Take the medicine.	☐	☐
9. I write with my right hand.	☐	☐
10. See you next week.	☐	☐

3 What happened?

Put the events in the right order. Read them all before you start.

A A nurse took an X-ray of Mark's arm.

B Mark went to the park.

C Mark got a prescription for some medicine.

D Mark went to see Dr Baker.

E Mark went back to see the doctor.

F Dr Baker and Mark looked at the X-ray pictures.

G Mark told the doctor what happened.

H Mark can play football again.

I Mark played football and fell on his arm.

1	2	3	4	5	6	7	8	9
B								

Tipp

Schau dir die Bilder genau an. Welche Wörter fallen dir ein, die du benutzen kannst, um die Bilder zu beschreiben?

1 What's the problem?

a) Write words for the pictures.

1.

A

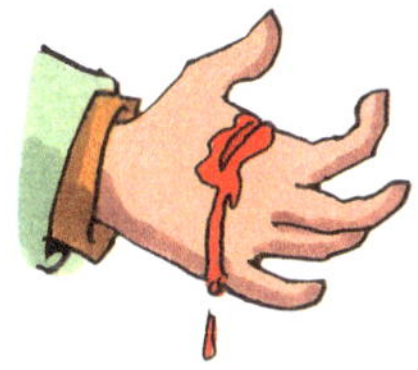

E

2.

B

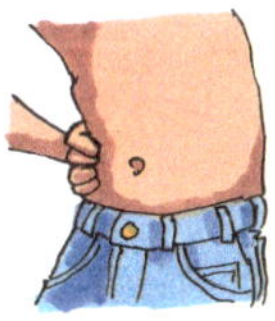

F

3.

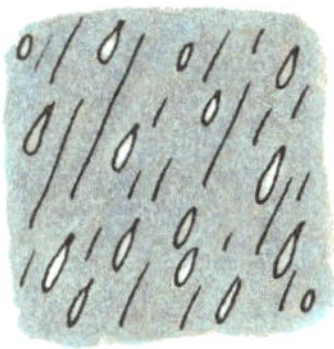

C

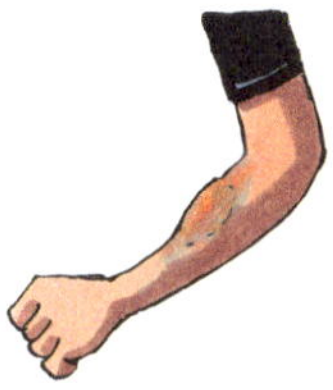

G

4.

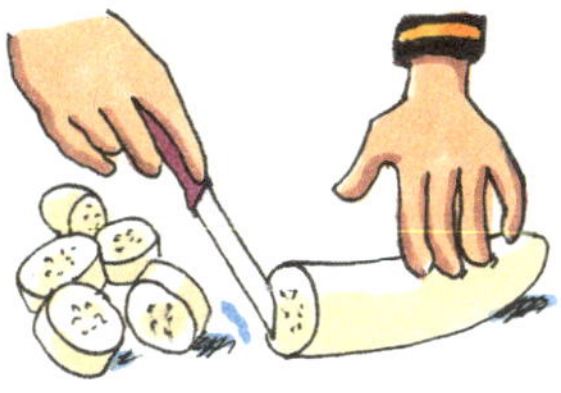

D

H

b) Match what happened and what advice the doctor gave the people (A-H) with the activities (1.-4.). You can use the advice more than once.

1	2	3	4

2 At the doctor's

Complete the dialogues between the doctor and the patients. They are the patients from exercise 1.

Dialogue 1

Dr Smith: Good morning. What's the problem?

Bob: I ate too much ______________ (1) yesterday. Now I have ______________ (2).

Dr Smith: Let me see. Does this hurt?

Bob: Ouch! Yes, it does.

Dr Smith: Then you should ______________ (3) and only drink ______________ (4) today. It should be better tomorrow.

Bob: Thank you Dr Smith.

Dialogue 2

Dr Smith: Good morning. ______________ (1)?

Anna: I ______________ (2) yesterday. My ______________ (3).

Dr Smith: It's just bruised. Here's a prescription for some ______________ (4). I'll put a ______________ (5) on it, too. Don't ride your bike for two weeks.

Anna: Thank you Dr Smith.

Dialogue 3

Dr Smith: Good morning. What's the problem?

Sam: I went hiking yesterday. The weather was ______________ (1).

Dr Smith: You have ______________ (2). You should ______________ (3) and drink ______________ (4).

Sam: Thank you Dr Smith.

Dialogue 4

Dr Smith: Good morning. ______________ (1)?

Paul: I ______________ (2) yesterday and I ______________ (3).

Dr Smith: Oh dear! Let me clean it for you. Here's a prescription for some ______________ (4). I'll put a ______________ (5) on it, too. Don't get it wet! Come again on Friday.

Paul: Thank you Dr Smith.

Language Tip

Wenn du sagen möchtest, was **unter bestimmten Bedingungen** geschehen wird oder geschehen kann, benutzt du einen **Bedingungssatz** (*if-clause*). Der *if*-Satz kann dabei als erstes oder als zweites stehen. Wenn der *if*-Satz zuerst kommt, setzt du ein Komma.

simple present	will-future	will-future	simple present
Bedingung:	**Folge:**	**Folge:**	**Bedingung:**
If we **have** a dog,	we **will play** with it.	I **will feel** better	if they **stop** arguing.
If the weather **is** bad,	we **won't go** out.	I **won't go** to school	if I **am** ill.

Video: WES-121583-005

1 If-clauses

a) Read the text and underline all the *if-clauses.*

Paul: Dad, you need to do some sport. If you do some sport, you won't feel tired.
Dad: You're right. If I go jogging in the park, I will listen to music, too.
Paul: That's a good idea. If you listen to music, you will have to be careful near the roads.
Dad: Very true, but I won't listen to loud music.
Paul: What about swimming, too? If you go swimming, I will come with you. I love swimming.
Dad: I don't know. I don't like swimming much. We could cook some healthy meals.
Paul: If I write a shopping list, will you buy the things after work?
Dad: Of course. What can we cook tomorrow?
Paul: If I have time after my homework, I'll look for a new recipe.
Dad: Great! Tomorrow after work, I can go shopping. If the weather is good, I will go jogging. Then we can cook together. That's a good plan.
Paul: OK, now I have to do my homework.

b) Write the if-clauses you found in a). Start your sentences with the result. You don't need the comma now.

1. You won't feel tired if you do some sport.
2. ______
3. ______
4. ______
5. ______
6. ______
7. ______

2 If ...

Complete the sentences with the right form of the verb in brackets.

1. If I ______________________ (play), our team ______________________ (win).
2. I ______________________ (ask) Anna for the recipe if I ______________________ (have) time.
3. If it ______________________ (rain), she ______________________ (not run) in the park.
4. We ______________________ (eat) pizza if we ______________________ (have) some cheese.
5. I ______________________ (go) to the doctor if I ______________________ (not feel) better.
6. If I ______________________ (get) a prescription, I ______________________ (get) some medicine.

3 Sentence chain

Use the next sentence to complete your sentence.

1. If you don't do any sport, you won't stay fit.
2. If you don't stay fit, ______________________
3. If you get ill, ______________________
4. If you go to the doctor, ______________________
5. If she gives you a prescription, ______________________
6. If you have to take some medicine, ______________________

If you aren't able to go to work, you will have to stay in bed.

4 Say it in English.

Write the sentences in English.

1. Wenn mein Bein morgen noch weh tut, werde ich zum Arzt gehen.

   ____

2. Wenn das Wetter schön ist, werden wir ein Picknick machen.

   ____

3. Wenn wir in den Urlaub fahren, werde ich jeden Tag Joggen gehen.

   ____

4. Wenn der Arzt mir einen Rat gibt, werde ich zuhören.

   ____

Audio: WES-121583-006

1 Anna, the football player

Listen to the interview. Are the sentences right or wrong? Tick ✓.

	right	wrong
1. Anna started playing football when she was six.	☐	☐
2. Anna played football with the boys in the park.	☐	☐
3. She was always in goal.	☐	☐
4. Anna's mum is her football trainer.	☐	☐
5. Emma played for England.	☐	☐
6. Anna has football practice on two days in the week.	☐	☐
7. Anna's parents worry about her school work.	☐	☐
8. Anna broke her leg two years ago.	☐	☐
9. Anna scored three goals in her first match when she was better.	☐	☐
10. Two goals are a hattrick.	☐	☐

2 What's wrong with Sarah?

Hi Sam, I can't come to football practice today. I ate too much pizza yesterday and I have a stomach ache. The doctor didn't give me a prescription. She told me to stay in bed and not do any sport. I can't go to school either. I have to eat toast and drink lots of tea – I don't like tea, but it's better than stomach ache. I hope I am better on Saturday and can play in the match. Anna has a broken arm (look at the photo she sent me) and can't play so I have to be fit. Please, tell the trainer I want to play football on Saturday. Thanks. ☺ Sarah

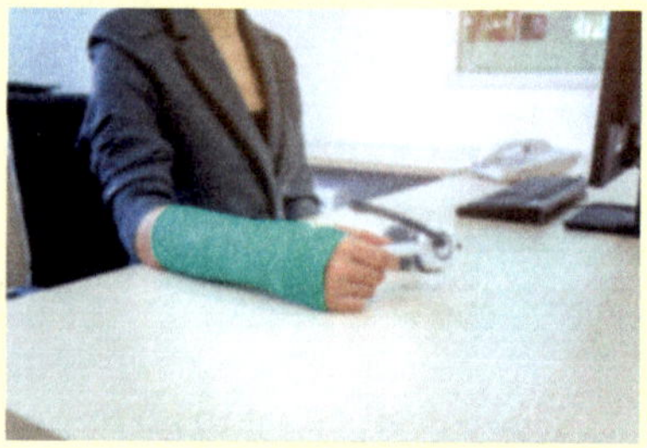

Read the text message and answer the questions. Write notes.

1. Where can't Sarah go? ______
2. When did she eat too much? ______
3. What did the doctor say? ______
4. What does Sarah have to eat and drink? ______
5. What is on Saturday? ______
6. What's wrong with Anna? ______

3 A healthy life

Complete the blog post about the things Paul did this week.

Hi everyone,

What a week! I have been really busy, but I feel really good. I got up early and went (1) ____________ in the park every day before school. I listened to my favourite (2) ____________ with my new earphones. I had a healthy breakfast, and I ate (3) ____________ for my lunch in the cafeteria at school, sometimes with chicken and sometimes with cheese. It was great. I didn't eat much (4) ____________, it was too hot. I played (5) ____________ with my friends in the playground after school and I didn't (6) ____________ any TV. I didn't miss it. Why don't you give it a try next week? Do more for your health and fitness and tell me about it.

Paul

4 If …

Cross out the wrong parts of the sentences.

1. If I am / will be ill, I go / will go to the doctor.
2. I tell / will tell the doctor where it hurts if she asks / will ask me.
3. I take / will take the prescription to the chemist if I get / will get one.
4. If I have to / will have to take tablets, I take / will take them.
5. If I can't do / won't do any sport, my sport friends understand / will understand.
6. My mum writes / will write a letter to my teacher if I can't go / won't go to school.
7. If I can't go / won't go to school, my teacher mails / will mail me my schoolwork.
8. If I miss / will miss a test, I write / won't write it at home.

Activities

Tipp

Schreibe deine Antworten mit Bleistift, dann kannst du sie einfacher korrigieren.

Audio: WES-121583-007

1 What people do …

What places do you hear? Tick ☑ the right things.

1. ☐

2. ☐

3. ☐

4. ☐

5. ☐

6. ☐

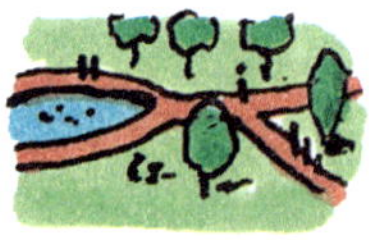

7. ☐

8. ☐

2 Who are they?

Match the speakers with what they do.

1. Mike
2. Chloe
3. Mr Brown
4. Suzie
5. David
6. Mrs Smith

A different things
B doctor
C helps people in hospital
D does the same things every day
E student (school)
F student (university)

1	2	3	4	5	6
B					

Tipp

Höre dir den Hörtext vor jeder Aufgabe nochmal an und danach ein weiteres Mal, um deine Antworten zu prüfen.

3 Complete the sentences.

Complete the sentences with the right words. There is one word you don't need.

doctor | dog | hospital | pub | school | university | way | work | young

1. Mike is a ____________ from London.
2. Chloe goes to ____________ in Cardiff.
3. Mr Brown is 70 and doesn't ____________ anymore.
4. Mr Brown played football on Sundays when he was ____________.
5. Suzie has a ____________ called Buddy.
6. David is a student at ____________.
7. Mrs Smith works in a ____________ on Sundays.
8. She helps people find their ____________ in the hospital.

4 Information about the speakers

Write two things that each person says about what he / she does.

1. Mike: ____________
2. Chloe: ____________
3. Mr Brown: ____________
4. Suzie: ____________
5. David: ____________
6. Mrs Smith: ____________

5 Over to you!

What do you do at the weekend? Write two things for each day.

Saturday: ____________

____

Sunday: ____________

____

Tipp

Um den Text besser zu verstehen, kannst du wichtige Textstellen unterstreichen.

Street Parties and celebrations

Hi everyone, here's Rosie. It's a weekend of celebrations this weekend. My town is 100 years old, and we are so happy. Yesterday there were street parties in nearly every street in my hometown. Everyone wore costumes. Some people were dressed like people 100 years ago, other people were dressed as fishermen as there are lots of fishermen in our town and others wore amazing hats as there is a big hat factory here. Lots of famous people come here to buy beautiful hats for special events.

Today there was a parade in the main street. There were a lot of bands and people dancing and lorries with scenes from places in and near our town. There were food stalls in the park with sweets, fish and chips, burgers, ice creams and so much more. There was a big fairground with a roller coaster, a big wheel, and many more fairground rides. I met my friends after the parade, and we went to the park. We had a great time and I won four free tickets to the train museum. Tomorrow there is no school, so we are going to go to the museum. I can't wait. What do the people in your town do when there is a celebration or special day? Let me know.

1 Celebration in town

Match the words with the pictures.

big wheel • costume • fish and chips • hat • lorry • tickets

1.

____

2.

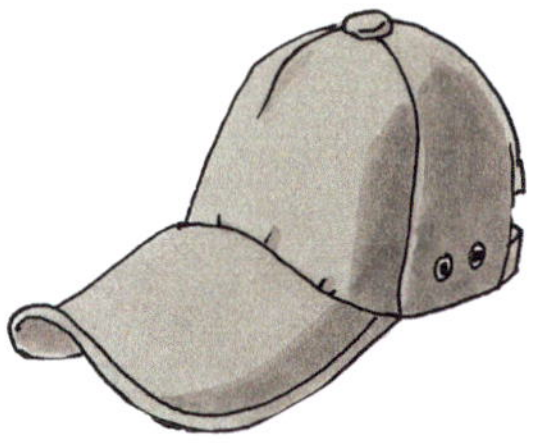

____

3.

____

4.

____

5.

____

6.

____

Tipp

Jetzt bearbeite diese Aufgaben. Lies den Blogeintrag noch einmal, um sicher zu gehen, dass du noch alles weißt.

2 About the celebration weekend

Match the sentence parts to make correct sentences about the blog post.

1. There are celebrations
2. Everyone wore costumes
3. There are fishermen and
4. People like beautiful
5. There were bands and
6. The food stalls
7. The fairground had
8. There is a
9. Rosie asks about

A people dancing at the parade.
B all weekend.
C celebrations in other towns.
D many rides.
E lots of hats in the town.
F hats for special events.
G train museum in the town.
H at the street parties.
I were in the park.

1	2	3	4	5	6	7	8	9
B								

3 Questions about the blog post

Answer the questions. Write complete sentences.

1. How old is the town? ______
2. What were people dressed as? ______
3. What is made in the town? ______
4. What could you eat from the food stalls? ______
5. Where were the tickets for? ______
6. Why can Rosie use the tickets the next day? ______
7. What does Rosie want people to do? ______
8. How would you answer Rosie's question? ______

______

Tipp

Lies alle Teile des Berichts, bevor du loslegst.

1 A newspaper report

a) Put the parts of the newspaper report in the right order.

A The weekend started off with the charity run. There were different distances for different age groups. The adults, over 18, had to run 10 kilometres. The weather was great, and Samira Jackson ran the best time.

B It rained on Sunday, so the tour of the museum was very popular.

C On Saturday afternoon the shops and stalls were busy. Everyone enjoyed the beautiful weather.

D After lunch the sun came out and everyone enjoyed the concert in the park.

E **What was on this weekend?**

F In the evening there was a disco in the sports hall. There was lots of different music, and everyone danced and had fun. It was a nice way to finish the first day of celebrations.

G A lot of people came to help tidy the town after a great weekend. Thank you.

H There were lots of food trucks and stalls from different school classes in the town centre. Everyone was so busy, and they were happy to have a drink and eat some food after the charity run.

1	2	3	4	5	6	7	8
E							

b) Write the report in the correct order.

2 Your newspaper report

a) Think about an event in your town and make notes.

When and what was the event? ______

Food and drink: ______

______

Events: ______

______

What was good/bad: ______

______

b) Write a newspaper report. Use your notes from a).

(You can stick a photo here or draw a picture to go with your newspaper report.)

Language Tip

Much (viel), ***many*** (viele) und ***a lot of*** (viel, viele) sind Mengenangaben, die man zusammen mit Nomen im Plural verwendet. Hierbei machst du einen Unterschied zwischen bejahten und verneinten Aussagen und Fragen.

In der Regel verwendest du ***a lot of*** (oder die informelle Variante ***lots of***) in **bejahten Aussagesätzen**. Bei **Verneinungen und Fragen** verwendest du ***many*** für **zählbare Nomen** (z. B. *bottles, eggs*) und ***much*** für **nicht zählbare Nomen** (z. B. *water, time*).

Aussagesätze:	They ate **a lot of** fruit.
Verneinung:	We didn't have **much** time to pack.
Fragen:	Do you have **many** friends?
	Do you eat **much** fruit?

Nach den Wörtern **too** und **so** verwendet man in bejahten Aussagesätzen auch **much** und **many**, z. B. **There was so much cake.**

Video: WES-121583-008

1 Quantities

a) Read the text and underline all the *quantities*.

Summer Activities in Watchet

There are a lot of things you can do this summer in Watchet. Our small town on the southwest coast of England has lots of activities and many of them are free.

There isn't much time to write your name on the lists and there are limited places for some of the activities.

There are many boats at Watchet. You can go on fishing trips, birdwatching or seal watching trips or you can help repair the boats – many of the owners need help all year.

There is a train museum in Watchet with a lot of old trains, old tickets and many other train things. It doesn't cost much money and you can spend all day in the museum. There is a café, too. Or you can help on the old train that takes a lot of visitors from Minehead to Taunton. You can check tickets or help in the restaurant kitchen.

If you like sport, there are many different sports activities. You can play football, rugby, hockey, go on bike tours of the area or learn to surf or sail a boat.

There is so much to do in Watchet you won't be bored this summer. Tell your friends and have fun. How many activities can you do? How much time have you got?

b) Find the right expressions in the text and write them down.

1. Es gibt viele Sachen, die du machen kannst. ______
2. Es kostet nicht viel Geld. ______
3. Wie viele Aktivitäten kannst du machen? ______
4. Wie viel Zeit hast du? ______

2 Much or many?

Put the words in the right group.

water | bottles | money | time | eggs | sugar | bread | people | activities | weight | sheep | sports

much	many

3 Activities week

What are the people saying? Cross out the wrong words.

1. Look at this list! How many / much / a lot of activities are there?
2. Many / Much / A lot of these activities are on the same day.
3. Does it say how many / much / a lot of they cost?
4. Look, many / much / a lot of the activities are in the swimming pool. I love swimming.
5. There aren't many / much / a lot of handicraft activities.
6. There isn't many / much / a lot of time between the activities on Friday.

4 Say it in English.

Write the sentences and questions in English.

1. Wir haben heute nicht so viel Zeit. ______
2. Wie viel Geld brauchst du für den Ausflug? ______
3. Wie viele Aktivitäten darfst du machen? ______
4. Nach dem Spaziergang am Strand hatte ich viel Sand in den Schuhen.
______
5. Ich kannte nicht so viele Menschen auf der Fahrradtour.
______

Audio: WES-121583-009

1 Gillian's weekend

Listen to Gillian. Put the information in the right order.

A They got up early and fed all the animals.

B Gillian went to the cinema.

C Gillian and Aunt Sandra's family ate some sandwiches.

D The 'Parade of the Farm Animals' started.

E Gillian went to Aunt Sandra's farm.

F They cleaned everything and made lots of cakes.

G The band stopped playing.

1	2	3	4	5	6	7

2 Sarah's blog post

Hi everyone,
What an amazing week of activities. On Monday we met at 7:30 a.m. (I didn't think I'd be there, but I was) and went on a coach to London. The weather was good, and we went on the London Eye. Then we visited the Tower of London. We had a special tour which was really interesting. On Tuesday we went to a food bank and helped the volunteers sort out the food. It came from supermarkets and restaurants. We put it in boxes and then delivered it to hostels for homeless people. We helped prepare meals for the homeless people and served the food. It was an interesting day, and it was great to help so many people. On Wednesday we were all really tired, but we enjoyed a boat trip on the Thames. We went home and had a lot to tell our families. Have you ever helped in a food bank or hostel for homeless people? Tell me about it.

Read the blog post and answer the questions. Write notes.

1. When did the coach leave? __________
2. What was the weather like? __________
3. What did Sarah do on the first day? __________
4. Who did Sarah help? __________
5. Did Sarah enjoy her time in London? __________
6. What did she do last in London? __________

3 A report

Complete the report. Use the information in the box.

celebration:	school's birthday
weather:	sun, rain
food:	salads, steaks, cakes, ice cream
events:	food trucks, competitions, presentations

The (1) ______________________ party

It was (2) ______________ weather to build the stands and prepare the school on Saturday morning. There were barbecues for (3) ______________ and tables with lots of (4) ______________ outside in the playground. In the music room there were tables of (5) ______________ for afternoon tea. There was also a man with (6) ______________ at the entrance with three other (7) ______________ . In the sports field there were (8) ______________ . Different classes had some great ideas. There were some really interesting (9) ______________ about school projects and trips in the school hall. The headteacher welcomed everyone and it started to (10) ______________ . It soon stopped and everyone had a great time.

4 Quantities

Complete the sentences with *much, many* or *a lot of.*

1. Look, there aren't ______________________ people in the museum.
2. Hurry up! We haven't got ______________________ time.
3. How ______________________ rackets do you need for a game of tennis?
4. There are ______________________ activities we can do here.
5. Don't spend ______________________ money on souvenirs and postcards.
6. How ______________________ sweets have you eaten?
7. How ______________________ do the activities cost?
8. There are ______________________ apples on the kitchen table.

Problems

Tipp

Manchmal kommt es auf die genauen Details an. Immer gut zuhören.

Audio: WES-121583-010

1 Brendon and Chris

What does Chris talk about? Tick ✓ the right things.

1. ☐

2. ☐

3. ☐

4. ☐

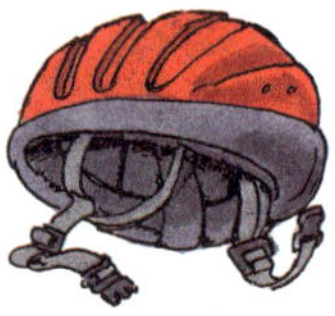

5. ☐

6. ☐

7. ☐

8. ☐

2 What happened?

Put the events in the right order.

A Chris said "Sorry".

B Chris almost knocked the cyclist off his bike.

C Chris left the house to walk to the bus stop.

D A cyclist was going fast and Chris didn't see him.

E The cyclist got off his bike and shouted at Chris.

F Chris got up.

G Chris and his new friends walked to the bus stop.

H Chris crossed the road.

I Rajiv and Charlie arrived and talked to the man.

1	2	3	4	5	6	7	8	9
F								

3 Answer the questions.

Choose the right answer(s) for each question. Tick ☑.

1. What is Chris's long name?
   - ☐ a) Christian
   - ☐ b) Christopher
   - ☐ c) Christof
2. Where is Chris from?
   - ☐ a) London
   - ☐ b) Beonstroke
   - ☐ c) Liverpool
3. When was the 'almost accident'?
   - ☐ a) On the first day of school.
   - ☐ b) On the last day of school.
   - ☐ c) In the holidays.
4. What did the cyclist take off?
   - ☐ a) his jacket
   - ☐ b) his gloves
   - ☐ c) his helmet
5. How did Chris feel?
   - ☐ a) happy
   - ☐ b) angry
   - ☐ c) scared
6. What does Chris think of Rajiv and Charlie?
   - ☐ a) They're cool.
   - ☐ b) They're great.
   - ☐ c) They're special.

4 All about Chris

Write as much information as you can about Chris.

Used to live in (3 pieces of information): ______________________________

____

Now lives in: ______________________________

Where he lives is: ______________________________

How he got to his old school: ______________________________

How he now gets to school: ______________________________

Likes: ______________________________

5 Over to you!

How do you get to school? Do you have to be careful like Chris? Write about your journey.

____

____

____

____

____

Tipp

Formelle und persönliche Briefe und E-Mails unterscheiden sich in der Sprache.

From: XXXXXXX

Reference: I need your help!

Dear Mark,

I have a big problem and I need your help.

I've always wanted a cat because I love animals. My mum says no because we live in a flat and don't have a garden. A cat needs to go outside. My parents both work and there is no one at home to let it out during the day. I can't have a dog because they are a lot of work. My mum is scared of mice, so I can't have a mouse as a pet. Rabbits are OK, but they don't do much. What can I do?

Jo, 14, Bristol

Dear Jo,

I understand your problem and I know everyone wants to have a pet. If there is no one at home it is unfair on a cat and your mum is right, a cat needs to go outside. Is there an animal home in your town? Why not take your parents and have a look? Maybe there is a dog that you like. Animal homes always want people to come and take the dogs for a walk. I know it isn't your pet, but it will make you happy and the dog.

Best, Mark

1 What's the problem?

Read the emails. Which pictures match Jo's email and the answer?

1. ☐

2. ☐

3. ☐

4. ☐

5. ☐

6. ☐

Tipp

Jetzt bearbeite diese Aufgaben. Lies die E-Mails noch einmal, um sicher zu gehen, dass du noch alles weißt.

2 Jo or Mark?

Who wrote what? Match the things with the right person.

	Jo	Mark
1. I need your help.	☐	☐
2. I understand your problem.	☐	☐
3. There is no one at home.	☐	☐
4. A cat needs to go outside.	☐	☐
5. I can't have a dog.	☐	☐
6. Maybe there is a dog.	☐	☐
7. Rabbits are OK.	☐	☐
8. What can I do?	☐	☐
9. Is there an animal home?	☐	☐
10. It will make you happy.	☐	☐

3 Questions about the emails

Answer the questions. Write complete sentences.

1. What pet does Jo want? ______
2. Where does Jo live? ______
3. What do Jo's parents do during the day? ______
4. What animals does Jo write about? ______
5. What does Mark talk about? ______
6. What can you do with dogs in animal homes? ______

4 Correct the sentences.

Correct the mistakes in the sentences.

1. Jo has a small problem. ______
2. Dogs aren't much work. ______
3. Cats can stay inside all day. ______
4. You can feed the animals in an animal home. ______

Tipp

Wenn du eine E-Mail liest, merke dir die Fragen, die der Absender stellt. In deiner Antwort beantwortest du die Fragen.

1 An email

a) Put the parts of the email in the right order.

A I keep getting horrible messages on my mobile phone. We shared our numbers in class, but I don't know who sends me the messages. Can I find out?

B From: Karim@xxx.com
Date: 21.08.20XX

C I want to keep my phone. If I tell my parents, will they take it off me? If I have a new …

D Please help me.
Karim, 14, Manchester

E I told my best friend about the messages, and she said I should tell my parents and our tutor. I'm scared to talk to my tutor. Will I be in trouble?

F Dear Sarah,

G number I will have to share it in the class. If the messages are from someone in my class, they will have my new number, too. What can I do?

H Can you help me, please? I have a big problem.

1	2	3	4	5	6	7	8
B							

b) Write the email in the correct order.

2 Your email

a) Read the email on page 38 again. Make notes about what Karim talks about and the questions he asks. Think of some of your own questions.

Information in email: ______________________

____

Karim's questions: ______________________

____

____

Your ideas: ______________________

____

b) Write your email to Karim. Use your notes from a).

Dear Karim,

____

____

____

____

____

____

____

____

____

____

____

____

____

____

____

____

____

____

____

____

Language Tip

Das ***past progressive*** funktioniert ähnlich wie das *present progressive*, nur dass es Vorgänge in der Vergangenheit (= *past*) beschreibt. Mit dem ***past progressive*** kannst du beschreiben:

a) was jemand zu einer bestimmten Zeit in der Vergangenheit **gerade tat** oder **was gerade passierte**.

b) **was gerade vor sich ging**, als (plötzlich) etwas anderes geschah bzw. diese Handlung unterbrach.

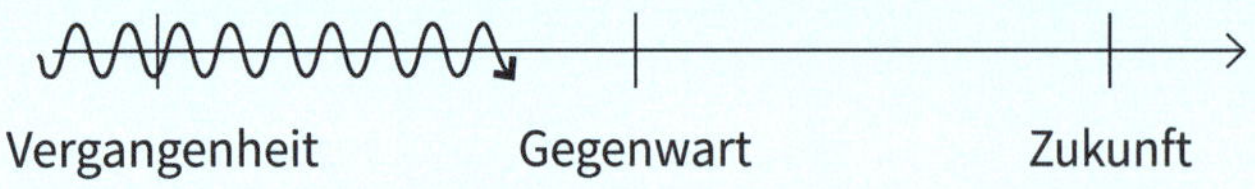

Du bildest das ***past progressive*** mit ***was*** oder ***were*** und dem **Verb in der ing-Form**. Bei Verneinungen hängst du ein ***not*** hinter ***was*** oder ***were***. Für Fragen stellst du ***was*** oder ***were*** an den Satzanfang bzw. hinter das Fragewort.

Aussagesatz:	**He was walking home.**	**We were talking to them.**
Verneinung:	**He wasn't walking home.**	**We were not talking to them.**
Fragen:	**When was he walking home?**	**Were you talking to them?**

Video: WES-121583-011

1 The past progressive

a) Read the text and underline all the verbs in the *past progressive*.

Dear Karen,

When I was talking to you last night there was a loud noise. Did you hear it? I thought it was the cat.

Me and Noah were looking for the cat and we found a mouse. It was eating some cheese under the table. The cat wasn't anywhere. Then we heard it. It wasn't happy.

We looked everywhere. Where was it sitting? Have a guess. It wasn't eating its food. It was hiding in the cupboard next to the table. It looked very scared.

"What are you doing?" Noah asked. The cat was happy to see us.

I think the cat was waiting to catch the mouse. The mouse saw the cat and closed the cupboard door.☺

What was the mouse doing after we found the cat? It was eating cheese under the table. I'm sure it was smiling.

Bye!

b) Look at the text in a) again and write down:

1. one positive statement with the *past progressive*:

____

2. one negative statement with the *past progressive*:

____

3. one question with the *past progressive*:

____

2 Was or were?

Complete the sentences and questions. Use *was* or *were*.

1. Sarah ______ talking to Karen.
2. The mouse ______ watching the cat.
3. Sarah and Noah ______ looking for the cat.
4. The cat and mouse ______ sitting in the kitchen.
5. What ______ you doing last night?
6. ______ your mum helping your dad?

3 Negative sentences

Write the sentences in exercise 2 (1-4) in the negative. Use *wasn't* or *weren't*.

1. ______
2. ______
3. ______
4. ______

4 What were they doing?

Put the words in the right order and write the questions for the answers.

1. phoned? | you | What | when | I | doing | were
   What were you doing when I phoned? – I was doing my homework.
2. doing | Anna | was | in | What | the | park?
   ______ – She was walking the dog.
3. morning? | Were | TV | this | watching | you
   ______ – No, I wasn't watching TV.
4. the | crisps? | Were | eating | friends
   ______ – Yes, they were eating crisps.
5. night? | was | doing | last | Anna | What
   ______ – She was playing a game.
6. a.m? | What | Sam | was | 12 | at | doing
   ______ – He was sleeping.

Audio: WES-121583-012

1 Robinson Crusoe

Listen to the interview. Match the information.

1. Professor Schwartz
2. Robinson Crusoe
3. Daniel Defoe
4. Alexander Selkirk
5. wild cats
6. Man Friday
7. children

A character in book from 1719
B frightened rats away
C rescued by Robinson Crusoe
D love Robinson Crusoe
E author of Robinson Crusoe
F East London University
G lived on an island for four years

1	2	3	4	5	6	7

2 Sam's problem

From: XXXXXXX
Reference: Re: Your problem

Hi Sam,
I understand your problem. It's always sad when parents split up. You're not alone. A lot of young people have the same problem and don't know what to do. First, write a list of questions you and your brother want to ask your parents. Then talk to your parents and try and find answers to things that worry you. Your parents will still be your parents when they split up and you need to deal with this as a family. Talk to friends whose parents have split up. They can help you, too. You can ask them questions you can't ask your parents. And remember your parents still love you and it isn't your fault.

Read the email and complete sentences.

1. Sam's parents are ____________________
2. Sam and his brother don't ____________________
3. First they should write ____________________
4. Then they should ____________________
5. They can also talk ____________________
6. They should remember ____________________

3 An email

Complete the email. Use the information in the box.

problem:	in love with best friend, can't say anything, has a new girlfriend
best friend:	likes sport, tall, brown hair, films
other:	tell him my feelings, spend time together, like new girlfriend

Dear Pam,

I have a problem. I'm in love with my (1) ______________ and I can't tell him. He is tall with (2) ______________ and blue eyes. We like the same (3) ______________ and go to the cinema every week and watch the newest (4) ______________ together. I wanted to tell him I really liked him, but I couldn't. Yesterday he told me he has a new (5) ______________ , and he is really happy. He wants her to come with us to the cinema. What can I do? Should I tell him about (6) ______________? I don't want to (7) ______________ with him and his new girlfriend. I don't want to (8) ______________ . Have I lost my best friend?

Sam, 14, London

4 Say it in English.

Write the sentences in English. Use the *past progressive*.

1. Sie sahen gerade einen guten Film im Fernsehen an.

____

2. Meine Freundin lief gerade im Park herum als sie mich sah.

____

3. Als ich aus dem Haus ging hat es nicht geregnet.

____

4. Als der Bus losfuhr, saßen wir nicht darin.

____

5. Was habt ihr gestern Abend gemacht?

____

Inventions

Tipp

Achte genau auf die Details.

Audio: WES-121583-013

1 Welcome to our village

What does Mark talk about? Tick ✓ the right things.

1. ☐

2. ☐

3. ☐

4. ☐

5. ☐

6. ☐

7. ☐

8. ☐

2 What is at the village?

Match the information.

1. buildings
2. a hundred years ago
3. special exhibitions
4. Spring Festival
5. Horse Festival
6. special programmes for school classes
7. village restaurant

A no electricity or modern technology
B work in fields without tractors
C drink, snack, special birthday
D use oven heated by a fire
E interesting pictures and objects
F flowers in gardens
G more than a hundred years old

1	2	3	4	5	6	7
G						

3 About the village

Are the sentences right or wrong? Tick ☑.

	right	wrong
1. There are over fifty buildings in the village.	☐	☐
2. There are farmhouses, an old school and an old church.	☐	☐
3. There is electricity and modern technology.	☐	☐
4. There are animals in the village in August.	☐	☐
5. There are interesting films at the special exhibitions.	☐	☐
6. You can drive a tractor at the Horse Festival.	☐	☐
7. You see what school life was like 100 years ago.	☐	☐
8. You can make bread and butter.	☐	☐
9. There are machines to make things easier.	☐	☐
10. There is a restaurant in the village.	☐	☐

4 Complete the sentences.

Complete the sentences with the right words.

1. Mark ______________ the visitors to the village.
2. The buildings came from other ______________.
3. Farmers lived in the ______________ with their families.
4. You will learn about the ______________ of life in the country.
5. There are special programmes for school ______________.
6. You can bake bread in an old oven that is heated by a ______________.
7. You can have a ______________ and a snack in the village restaurant.
8. You can celebrate a special ______________ in the village restaurant.

5 Over to you!

Have you been to an interesting place or museum? Write about it.

Where? ______________

When? ______________

Who with? ______________

Liked: ______________

Didn't like: ______________

Tipp

Der Titel und das Bild helfen dir, den Text zu verstehen.

The Transport Museum

Our museum has something for everyone – even if you don't like cars.

Start on the top floor and listen, read and watch all about the history of cars. When was the first one made and where? How much did it cost to buy? Who had one?

The third floor is all big road vehicles. That's coaches and lorries. What did they look? What did they move? How big were they?

Air travel is on the second floor. There are planes and helicopters. You can sit in them, try and fly one in a simulator or build one out of paper.

Then the first floor is full of bikes and motorbikes. There are some with two wheels, some with three wheels and some with lots of wheels. You can give them a try.

Water is the theme on the ground floor. Why do boats stay above water? Sit in one and sail.

And when you're hungry or just need a break, there is a café, snack bar or restaurant on each floor. They match the transport on each floor. There is a shop before you leave the museum. You can buy posters, postcards, pens, books and films about the museum.

There are audio guides or tour guides to help you in the museum. The museum is free.

1 The transport museum

What are the things? Write the names under the pictures.

1. 

____

2. 

____

3. 

____

4. 

____

5. 

____

6. 

____

Tipp

Lies den Text noch einmal, um sicher zu gehen, dass du noch alles weißt. Dann kannst du die Aufgaben lösen.

2 About the museum

Match the things with the right places in the museum.

1. snack bars
2. shop
3. cars
4. boats
5. bikes
6. planes
7. coaches
8. lorry
9. simulator

A Top floor
B 3rd floor
C 2nd floor
D 1st floor
E Ground floor

1	2	3	4	5	6	7	8	9

3 Questions about the museum

Answer the questions. Write notes.

1. Who is the museum for? ______
2. Where are the road vehicles? ______
3. What can you make? ______
4. What can you try? ______
5. Can you sit in a plane and a boat? ______
6. Where can you eat something? ______
7. What can you buy in the shop? ______
8. Who can you ask questions? ______
9. How many floors does the museum have? ______
10. How much does the museum cost? ______

Tipp

Lies alles gut durch und schau dir die Bilder an, bevor du anfängst zu schreiben.

1 Inventions

a) Match the information.

1. Thomas Edison, USA
   light bulb
2. Karl Benz, Germany
   car
3. Josephine Cochrane, USA
   dishwasher
4. John Walker, England
   matches
5. Alexander Graham Bell, Scotland
   telephone
6. Ruth Wakefield, USA
   chocolate chip cookies

A make fire
1826

B light rooms and streets
1879

C make your sweet tooth happy
1930

D wash plates, cups and glasses
1886

E travel long distances
1876

F talk to people far away
1876

1	2	3	4	5	6

b) Write the inventions under the photos.

1. 

____

2. 

____

3. 

____

4. 

____

5. 

____

6. 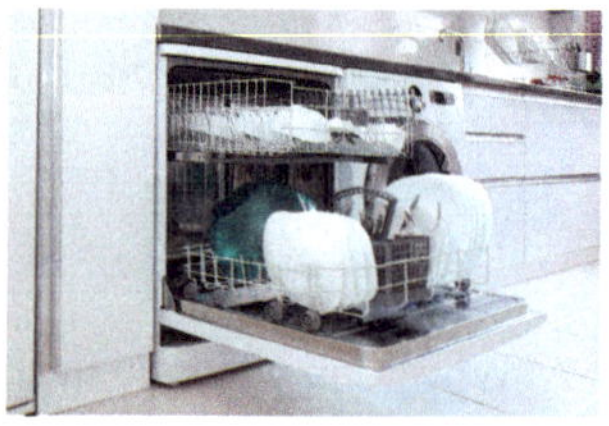

____

2 About the inventions

a) Write three sentences about each invention on page 48.

1.

2.

3.

4.

5.

6.

b) Find out about another invention. Write a short text. Write about:

Who invented it? | When was it invented? | What does it do? | What do you think of it?

Language Tip

Sätze im Aktiv sagen uns, wer oder was handelt. Wenn es aber nicht wichtig oder klar ist, wer etwas tut oder getan hat, kannst du das **Passiv** verwenden.

Das **Passiv** bildest du mit einer **Form von *be*** + **Partizip Perfekt (3. Form des Verbs)**. Das heißt, du setzt praktisch immer die Form von ***be*** in die richtige Zeit und setzt dahinter das Partizip Perfekt des Verbs.

Beispiele:	**simple present**	**simple past**
	English **is spoken** all over the world.	Latin **was spoken** in Athens.
	Cars **are bought** by adults.	Cars **were invented** a long time ago.

Video: WES-121583-014

1 The passive

a) Read the text and underline all the verbs in the *passive*.

Cars

The first car was invented in 1672. Then different inventors tried different ideas and in 1887 Carl Benz developed a car and several of them were made. In 1908 the Ford Motor Company produced the Ford Model T which was the first car made in a big factory. Lots of people worked on assembly lines[1]. Many of the same car were made every day.

People wanted to travel, and they all wanted a car. Cars were bought in their thousands and roads were built everywhere.

Nowadays electricity is used instead of petrol. This protects the environment. Cars are used a lot, maybe we should all walk more.

b) Find the *passive* sentences for these *active* sentences.

1. He invented the first car in 1672. ______
2. Carl Benz made several cars. ______
3. They built many of the same car every day. ______
4. Many people bought a car. ______
5. Workers built roads everywhere. ______
6. Nowadays cars use electricity. ______
7. We use cars a lot. ______

[1] assembly line – Fließband

2 Past participles

What are the past participles of these irregular verbs?

1. bring: ______________________
2. drink: ______________________
3. eat: ______________________
4. get: ______________________
5. give: ______________________
6. go: ______________________
7. have: ______________________
8. know: ______________________
9. make: ______________________
10. put: ______________________
11. take: ______________________
12. write: ______________________

3 What do you know?

Complete the sentences with the *past participle* of the verbs in the box and the *simple present*.

build	buy	catch	drive	make	use

1. Cakes ______________________ with butter, sugar, flour and eggs.
2. Stamps ______________________ on letters.
3. Food ______________________ in supermarkets.
4. Cars ______________________ by people over 18.
5. Roads ______________________ to connect towns.
6. Fish ______________________ in rivers and the sea.

4 Famous inventions

Complete the sentences with the *past participle* of the verbs in the box and the *simple past*.

build	develop	invent	invent	speak	use	wash

1. The light bulb ______________________ first to light rooms and streets.
2. People ______________________ to on the telephone for the first time in 1876.
3. Matches ______________________ by John Walker.
4. Cars ______________________ to travel long distances on roads.
5. Plates ______________________ by hand before dishwashers ______________________.
6. Mobiles ______________________ so you can take them with you.

Audio: WES-121583-015

1 Important inventions

Listen to the podcast. Match the inventors with the right invention and right year.

A television

1. Alexander Graham Bell
2. Thomas Edison
3. John Logie Baird

B telephone
C light bulb
D 1876
E 1926
F 1879

1	2	3

2 The best smartphone

The best smartphone
Check this smartphone out. I can't believe how good it is. I take photos that are amazing. It is easy to use, and I don't lose my photos or films. I can send them to all my friends and post them on the internet, too. It is a lovely colour – my favourite – white. The noises it makes when I get a message are cool, I can also save my own music. And guess what? I can make phone calls – that isn't something I do very often, but it is good to know it has that app, too. ☺

Read the information and answer the questions. Write complete sentences.

1. What is the text about? ______
2. What is amazing? ______
3. What don't you lose? ______
4. What colour is it? ______
5. What can you save? ______
6. What else can you do with it? ______

3 A great invention

Complete the text with the words in the box.

behind	black	change	colour	films	living room	small	stream	television	watch

I (1) ______________ this invention every day. There is a big one in our (2) ______________ and my brother has a (3) ______________ one in his bedroom. You (4) ______________ the channels with a remote control. I can never find it. It's usually (5) ______________ a cushion on the sofa. We watch series and also (6) ______________ on it. We also (7) ______________ football matches and formula one races on it. Can you guess what this great invention is? Yes, it is the (8) ______________. It was invented in 1926 by John Logie Baird from Scotland. The pictures were (9) ______________ and white at first. Now everything is (10) ______________. What would we do without this invention?

4 Inventions you know

Complete the sentences with the verbs in the *passive* of the *simple present* or the *simple past*.

1. Windows ______________ (make) of glass.
2. Computers ______________ (sell) everywhere.
3. Apps ______________ (upload) onto mobile devices.
4. The telephone ______________ (invent) in 1876.
5. Our television ______________ (buy) last year.
6. Our house ______________ (build) in 2000.
7. Microwaves ______________ (use) to warm food.
8. My bike ______________ (steal) from the park.

Holidays

Tipp

Höre genau zu, was Adrian erzählt. Schau dir die erste Aufgabe an und dann höre Adrian ein zweites Mal zu. Dann nimm einen Stift und löse die erste Aufgabe.

Audio: WES-121583-016

1 Which summer camp is right for you?

What does Adrian talk about? Tick ✓ the right things.

1. ☐

2. ☐

3. ☐

4. ☐

5. ☐

6. ☐

2 Which summer camp is it?

Match the activities with the right summer camp.

1. Sports camp
2. Film making camp
3. Art camp
4. All camps

A work with stone and other things
B bedtime rules
C practise your favourite sport
D learn to use a camera
E take home nice things
F train and play matches
G write stories
H listen to everyone

1	2	3	4
C,			

3 Answer the questions.

Answer the questions with information you hear about the summer camps.

1. Where are the summer camps Adrian talks about? ______
2. Who often organises traditional sports camps? ______
3. Who did Adrian go to a training camp with? ______
4. Where did Adrian take the train to? ______
5. What can you do with your films after the summer camp? ______
6. What can you do with your photos at the Art camp? ______
7. What do you have to do with your room? ______
8. What should you never do at the camp? ______

4 Information about summer camps

Complete the information about the summer camps.

1. Sports camp

   Others there: ______

   Activities: ______

   ______

2. Film making camp

   Others there: ______

   Activities: ______

   ______

3. Art camp

   Others there: ______

   Activities: ______

   ______

5 Over to you!

Have you ever been to a summer camp? Write about it.

What kind of summer camp was it? ______

Where was it? ______

When was it? ______

Tipp

Lies alle Texte durch, bevor du mit den Aufgaben anfängst.

London
The capital of England and a city full of sights for everyone. From museums about history and science to skyscrapers with views of the city or buildings that everyone knows from the TV or just sitting in a park watching life. Food is also not a problem in London, there is something for everyone. Come and see.

Loch Ness
Everyone has heard of Loch Ness, but it is more than a lake. There are mountains to hike in, parks to visit, lakes to fish in and restaurants where you can enjoy typically Scottish food. Of course, you can also look for Nessie. You can be as active or relaxed as you want. Take time out from city life or just from life itself. You'll love it here.

Cornwall
What can be better than the southwest coast of England? There are parks, beaches, castles, cream teas, fishing trips and so much more. There are cities if you miss the shops and want to go shopping. The Cornish people always have a smile for you. Stay in a hotel or holiday cottage, Cornwall has everything.

1 Holidays

Read about the holiday places. Match the right picture to each place.

1.

____

2.

____

3.

____

2 Anna's holiday

Read what Anna likes. Which place is best for her holiday?

Hi, my name's Anna. I love sport and I'm always busy. My friends don't understand why I love walking everywhere. It's good for the environment and I keep fit. It's also free. ☺
What do I do on holiday? I walk and I walk. I also like history, but not every day. It's nice to visit a castle or a museum, but I need to be outside walking or hiking in the fresh air the next day. I also love food – I need to eat lots so I can walk so much. I like to try new things and eat food that is typical of where I am. I don't like shopping and I buy everything online. I always find what I need.

The best place for Anna' s holiday is ____.

Tipp

Lies die Texte über die Urlaubsorte noch einmal, um sicher zu gehen, dass du noch alles weißt.

2 Which holiday place?

Match the things with the right places. Some things go with more places.

1. London
2. Loch Ness
3. Cornwall

A history
B fishing
C parks
D cream teas
E skyscrapers
F mountains
G shopping
H museums
I lake

1	2	3
		A,

4 Questions about the holidays

Answer the questions. Write complete sentences.

1. What can you see from a London skyscraper? ______
2. Where do you know London buildings from? ______
3. Who has no problems with the food in London? ______
4. What is Loch Ness? ______
5. Where can you eat typically Scottish food? ______
6. What can you take time out from? ______
7. Where is Cornwall? ______
8. What are there in the Cornish cities? ______
9. Where can you stay in Cornwall? ______
10. Which place would you choose for a holiday? ______

Tipp

In einem Blogeintrag kannst du anderen von deinen Erfahrungen und Erlebnissen erzählen.

1 A blog post

a) Put the parts of the blog post in the right order.

A I want to spend my holidays at home, but I don't want to be bored. I'm going to do lots of activities.

B After a week of French I will need some sport. There is an activities week at the sports club and there are lots of different sports to try. I had lots of questions and the trainers helped me choose the best activities before I registered.

C Tell me about your holiday plans. Where are you going? What do you want to see? How did you plan everything?

D Then I'm going to school for a week. I need to practise my French and there is a free course at school. We will do lots of talking, but also watch French films and cook French food together. It sounds great.

E Best, Sam

F So that is what I'm going to do in my summer holidays.

G I have looked on different websites and I know what is happening in my hometown. First, I'm going to spend a week as a volunteer in the local animal home. They need help walking the dogs.

H My friends will be back from their holidays after the activity week, and we can have fun together.

1	2	3	4	5	6	7	8
A							

b) Write the blog post in the correct order.

Tipp

Menschen, die deinen Blogeintrag lesen, können ihn auch kommentieren.

2 A blog post comment

a) Read the blog post on page 58 again and this comment. Now answer the questions.

Comments:
speedy#3, 08.20XX: Your hometown sounds great fun and there is so much to do. There is so much to do for young people, and you got so much help. I think it is great to do a mixture of fun things, do something to help your school marks and also help others. I think only a week at the animal home might be hard – I'm not sure I could leave the animals after only a week. I guess they also need help in school time, and you could walk the dogs on a Saturday, too.

1. What does the blogger ask at the end of the blog post?

____

2. Are the questions answered in the comment?

____

3. What is important when you write a comment? Think about how it is written.

____

4. What is the idea at the end of the comment?

____

b) Now write your own comment to the blog post on page 58. Try to answer the blogger's questions.

____

____

____

____

____

____

____

____

____

Language Tip

Mit **Modalverben** (Modal = Art und Weise) kannst du ausdrücken, was jemand **(nicht) kann**, **(nicht) darf**, **(nicht) machen soll** oder **(nicht) machen muss**.

Ist was **erlaubt** oder **möglich**, so kannst du *can* (können) sowie die Ersatzformen *be allowed to* (dürfen) oder *be able to* (die Fähigkeit haben) verwenden. **Verbote** drückst du mit *can't* (nicht können) und *not be allowed to* (nicht dürfen) aus. Mit *must not* drückst du ein **starkes Verbot** aus.

Beispiele: I can eat sweets. He wasn't allowed to drink coke.

Must heißt **müssen**. Meist kannst du es auch durch *have to / has to* ersetzen. Wenn du sagen willst, dass jemand etwas **nicht tun muss**, verwendest du *don't / doesn't have to*. Mit *should* (sollen) und *should not* (nicht sollen) drückst du eine **Empfehlung** aus.

Achtung:
Must not (mustn't)
klingt wie nicht müssen,
heißt aber nicht dürfen!

Beispiele: I *have to* eat healthy food. We *shouldn't* eat so much sugar.

Video: WES-121583-017

1 Modal verbs

a) Read the text and underline all the *modal verbs*.

I'm really looking forward to our holiday. Scotland is a special place. We just have to remember there are rules there: in the museums and castles, in the hotels and also in restaurants. Of course, I know in restaurants you should be quiet and polite to everyone. In museums and castles, you shouldn't run or shout, you should only eat and drink in the special areas and you aren't allowed to take photos in some places. In the last hotel we stayed in I was allowed to look in the kitchen and I was able to watch the cook, that was fun. I wasn't allowed to cook any food for hotel guests. I'd like to be a cook when I leave school.

b) Complete the lists with the things from the text that Samira can do or can't do.

Things Samira can do	Things Samira can't do

2 The right word

Cross out the wrong words. Sometimes more than one is correct.

1. Mathew broke his leg, and he couldn't / has to / can do any sports on holiday.
2. This picture is very expensive. You can / must / mustn't be very careful.
3. Daniel ate too much breakfast and he couldn't / wasn't able to / mustn't eat any lunch.
4. My brother is 10. He isn't allowed to / can't / haven't to go in a pub in Scotland.
5. Claire is going on holiday. She has to / have to / isn't allowed to pack her bag.
6. You have to / mustn't / aren't allowed to do that. It's too dangerous.

3 What are the rules?

Write sentences with (*not*) *allowed to*.

1. No chocolate before lunch, Mark!

4. Quiet please, Sarah! No music after 10 o'clock!

2. Sorry kids, no chips in the shop!

5 You can't use your mobile phones in the restaurant!

3. You're welcome to come and look around the garden!

6 Mark, you can have a piece of cake, but only one!

1. Mark isn't allowed to eat chocolate before lunch.
2. ______
3. ______
4. ______
5. ______
6. ______

Audio: WES-121583-018

1 Airport announcements

Complete the tables with the missing information about the flights.

Destination	Departure time	Gate	Information
Paris	1. ________	17B	–
2. ________	15.07	8M	cancelled
Madrid	12.05	3. ________	delayed by 60 minutes
Frankfurt	4. ________	1A	on time

From	Arrival time	Information
Washington D.C.	–	5. ________ late
New York	6. ________	Mr Brown to information
Cologne	–	delayed by 7. ________
8. ________	15.30	delayed by 6 hours

2 Sarah's postcard

Read the postcard and answer the questions. Write notes.

> Hi Sam,
> We're having a great holiday here in Wales. There is so much to do. We went to Cardiff and visited the castle and the stadium. We went hiking in the mountains and tomorrow we're going fishing in the sea. I hope the weather is nice and the sea is flat. We can cook and eat any fish we catch. We'll be hungry if we don't catch any fish. ☹ I love fish … with chips.
> See you soon,
> Sarah

1. Who is the postcard to? ________
2. Where is Sarah? ________
3. What did she do in Cardiff? ________
4. What did she do in the mountains? ________
5. Where is she going tomorrow? ________
6. What does she love? ________

3 A blog post

Complete the blog post. Use the information in the box.

What?	World Swimming Championships
Where?	local swimming pool
When?	weekend
Problems?	looked too old, child in seat – not move (ice cream)

Hi everyone.

Let me tell you about my (1) ______________________. I went to the World Swimming Championships at my local (2) ______________________. They were amazing. So, I had some problems getting in. They didn't believe I was a student – I look (3) ______________________. I bought a drink and an ice cream and went to find my seat. When I got to my (4) ______________________, there was a child sitting there. Her parents said it was her seat and she (5) ______________________. Then her parents arrived and saw it was the wrong seat. I gave her my (6) ______________________ and sat down. The swimming was great. What did you do at the (7) ______________________? Was it fun? Were there any (8) ______________________?

4 Say it in English.

Write the sentences in English. Use *modal verbs*.

1. Du solltest keine Fotos machen.

____

2. Wir dürfen auf keinen Fall Pommes frites im Schloss essen.

____

3. Dürfen wir angeln gehen?

____

4. Wir müssen in den Bergen auf den Wegen bleiben.

____

5. Ich darf keinen Sand vom Strand mit nach Hause nehmen.

____

6. Ich kann Englisch und Französisch sprechen.

____

Bildquellen

|Alamy Stock Photo, Abingdon/Oxfordshire: Wayman, Richard 62.1; Westend61 GmbH / Weinhäupl, Wolfgang Titel. |Imago, Berlin: ITAR-TASS 46.1. |iStockphoto.com, Calgary: deepblue4you 48.4; Devonyu 48.1; Yurdakul Gundogdu, Omer 48.6. |Shutterstock.com, New York: marcociannarel 53.1; Padmayogini 15.1. |stock.adobe.com, Dublin: Africa Studio 48.2; Baker, Darren 60.1; Bueckert, Axel 48.5; DigitalGenetics 48.3; Moraiti, Konstantinos 50.1; Orion Media Group 30.1; Ozerova, Alena 52.1; ttanothai 22.1.

Trackliste

Alle Audios und Videos können auf der Homepage www.westermann.de/webcode mit dem im Heft vermerkten Webcode (z. B. WES-121583-001) abgespielt werden.

Kapitel	Seite	Aufgabe	Webcode
1	4	1	WES-121583-001
1	10	Language tip	WES-121583-002
1	12	1	WES-121583-003
2	14	1	WES-121583-004
2	20	Language tip	WES-121583-005
2	22	1	WES-121583-006
3	24	1	WES-121583-007
3	30	Language tip	WES-121583-008
3	32	1	WES-121583-009
4	34	1	WES-121583-010
4	40	Language tip	WES-121583-011
4	42	1	WES-121583-012
5	44	1	WES-121583-013
5	50	Language tip	WES-121583-014
5	52	1	WES-121583-015
6	54	1	WES-121583-016
6	60	Language tip	WES-121583-017
6	62	1	WES-121583-018